TRUE
TIDES

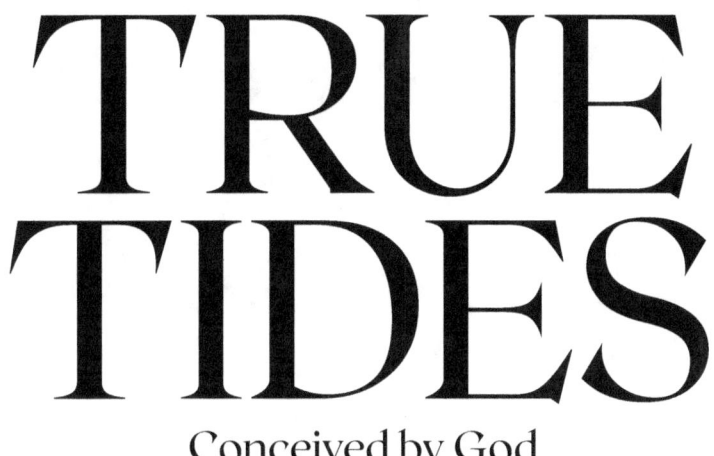

TRUE TIDES

Conceived by God

Get Ready For A New Life's Perspective ...

Managing your time and value by God's Standard!

DR. MARCI TILGHMAN BRYANT

ISBN: 978-1-963068-39-9 (sc)
ISBN: 978-1-963068-40-5 (e)

Library of Congress Control Number: 2024905154

TRUE
TIDES

A READING ADVENTURE

A WRITING ADVENTURE

A PRAYER JOURNAL ADVENTURE

THIS BOOK/JOURNAL IS AN ADVENTURE INTO THE WORLD THAT GOD HAS DESIGNED FOR YOU AND ME SO THAT WE MAY LIVE THE BEST LIFE HERE IN THE EARTH WHILE PREPARING FOR ETERNITY!

TABLE OF CONTENTS

DEFINITION

The definition of TRUE:
  a. Being in accordance with the actual state or status or condition of a thing
  b. Conforms to actual reality or facts

The definition of TIDES:
  a. The rise and fall of water levels, (sea, oceans, streams, ponds, etc as a result of gravity/gravitational pulls via the sun, mood, wind, etc

There are High Tides	There are Morning Tides
There are Low Tides	There are Evening Tides
There are Light Tides	There are Dark Tides

Knowledge and wisdom is needed to move successfully through life's journey. There are many teachers that come and go, but only ONE who has always been, always is, and always will be ...

DECLARATION

TEACH ME LORD & I shall be taught!
LEAD ME LORD & I shall be led!
FEED ME LORD & I shall be fed!
WITH YOUR WORD ....
I shall be ...
HEALTHY! WEALTHY! WISE!
& Always abounding in the work that you have created me for and called me to ...

At least 60% of the human body mass is Water I One Response: "I didn't know"
Another Response: You don't say"
Still another Response: "I am glad that NOW I know" ...

ACKNOWLEDGEMENT

The spirit of the living and almighty God moves constantly & consistently throughout the universe of which He has created.

He makes known His will to His creation through the ages by His uncompromising word, angels and dreams and prophets. He moves upon our senses and our souls and the human spirit to communicate His message(s) to mankind.

He spoke to me in a dream and gve me the title and direction that this journal should take. It is to be an adventure to change one's life by taking him/her through a series of thought provoking and mind changing events. It is to challenge

I SHALL BE AND I AM ... HEALTHY, WEALTHY, AND WISE ACCORDING TO THE WORD OF GOD!

Several years ago I was tested in the area of my faith as it concerned money. I had been ill for almost a year, unable to work on a steady basis. Bills were due and funds were low. I turned to prayer; and picked up the bible. I read many verses until I came upon two that I would grasp and hold onto for dear life. The first one was "If I delight myself in the Lord He will give me the desires of my heart". I desired to be out of debt. I desired to be able to pay my bills on time and also to even eliminate some of them altogether. Next, the scripture that I latched onto was "In all thy ways acknowledge Him and He shall direct my path". I needed to know where to go and what to do to correct this situation. I put all my faith into those words and then spoke out loud ... I shall not only hear this word, this instruction but I declare to follow it and believe that it will lead me away from this lack of ability to pay my bills. And I will never be broke again!" God opened two doors for me to get the income I needed to be financially solvent again. From that day even unto now I have and will continue to have enough and even more than enough to meet my needs. Why? Because God will always make a way for me should I follow His lead.

I will keep faith in His methods, not my own. My part is to be obedient to His word.

So, no matter what the situation is that you find yourself in, take a good look as to how God has equipped you and ask Him to direct your path. Ask Him to show you the open door that you can walk through to change your situation.

OPENING PRAYER

Our Father (Our Father) which art in heaven,
Hallowed be thy name,
Thy Kingdom come,
Thy will be done on earth as it is in heaven.
Give us (me) this day our (my) daily bread,
And forgive us (me) our (my) trespasses
as we Forgive those who trespass against us (me).
Lead us (me) not into temptation
but deliver us (me) from evil
for thine is the kingdom and the power
and the glory forever.
AMEN

PERSPECTIVE

Under the direction of the Holy Spirit, I have been led to make known a few thoughts and goals for this book/journal. And to this end I was given directions as to add the comments of six other individuals so that their perspective may touch readers a well.

My Perspective: *Dr Marci Tilghman Bryant*

The Spirit of the living and Almighty God moves constantly and consistently throughout the universe of which He has created.

He makes known His will to His creation through the ages by His uncompromising word, His angels and dreams. He moves upon our senses and our souls and the human spirit to communicate His Message{s) to mankind.

God spoke to me in a dream and gave the title and the direction that this book/journal should take. I chose to walk in obedience.

It is to be an adventure to change your life by taking you through a series of thought provoking and mind changing activities from the carnal perspective to the spiritual perspective. Then you make the choice of which path you will use your "free will" to follow.

Choose the path that God has designed for you and you will forever be in keeping with your **TRUE TIDE!**

PERSPECTIVE #2: *Harry Hamil*

As a small boy, I was told that God made all people. I was also taught about heaven and hell and that if people were bad they would not go to heaven. When I heard about how the devil uses everything God made against us it made me sad. I knew nothing about man being made of more than 60% water. I listened very carefully when I was told about "tides"; how they flow back and forth. I got a picture in my mind about how the devil pulls people back and forth trying to get them to do wrong against each other and God. I made up my mind that I didn't want that kind of life being pulled back and forth. I want to believe God's word and do what it says without being compromised. I want to be true to my fellowman and to my God.

PERSPECTIVE #3: *Sister Darlene Willis*

Being a member of Building the Virtuous Temple Outreach Ministries (BVT) has taught me how to become more rooted and grounded in the Lord God through seminars, workshops, plays and education via faithbased college degree programs. My spiritual ears listening for the voice of God to guide my every footstep has become very important in my life. I love the beaches, being around water brings a certain calm to my experience. We are to be fishers of men, thus I find it fascinating to watch the tides flow back and forth from the shoreline, thinking about how we are instruments that God can use as the tide to draw others to Himself. But we also have an enemy that uses that same tide to try to draw others away from God. I understand the high tides and the low tides. What we do not want nor, desire to do in a tide that was not ordered by God may lead to us go wading in high waters, more than we can handle. A low tide is more manageable but either way we need God with us. His influence keeps us through the whole of everything we face. God wants us to be careful as He does not want us to become caught in a rip tide. When the devil is present rip tides are present.

They take us further out to sea, away from the area of safety that God intends for us to operate. Rip tides are intended to steer us away from the goal, that's what the devil wants ... us to fail in our mission. Thus, he goes after the part of our being, our flesh, that connects us to the tide that flows back and forth, to and from. Rip tides can gather trash and filth in its currents. They can create havoc where there should be none. Often they are hard to clean up. Only our enemy wants to take us away from what's good, or put us in damaging situations before putting us on a path that is not good for our soul and spirit. True tides embodies God's best for us always.

PERSPECTIVE #4 - *Sister Arnetta Davis*

I enjoy listening to the word being taught, especially when the speaker gives a new way of understanding what I already know about the word. Hearin the pastor speak on 'true tides ', helped me to feel good about holding onto the truth in all situations; even when I don't want to hear it. I know God's way is the right way, but sometimes I couldn't understand why I could be so easily swayed away from truth. My flesh makes is so easy sometimes to give in to what I know I shouldn't. So when I make up my mind to do what's right it gets easier because I know also that I am not alone. I have the Holy Spirit and my Christian family right here with me. I thank God. It has taken years for me to get to where I am in my spiritual growth, so I plan to do what I need to do to stay committed.

PERSPECTIVE #5 - *Elder Clarence (Pete) Tilghman, Jr*

True tides. Exactly what comes to my mind when I hear these words. The definition of the word true can be defined as "Fact", also "Reality". You can define "Tides" as the rise and fall of water as a result of gravitational pull(s). Now God has called His creation to obey, the precious words that He has moved upon the hearts of men to write in the Bible. Now speaking from a parent's perspective, when you have kids, they are rewarded for their obedience. God does the same with us, His own creation. Usually obedience reap acceptable and positive rewards, whereas disobedience reap punishment and unwanted consequences; thus the word "True" meaning "Fact" or "Reality". Now the "Tides" with the body being at least 60% water is dealing with the flow and ups and downs of life. High tides is up; Low tides is being down. How you operate determines your true tides, either high or low. And it should be noted that the tides can and do change according to the "pulls" of life and which pull you lean toward. Thus you decide your "true" and your "tides" high or low.

PERSPECTIVE #6 - *Elder Stacy Stance/I*

On Saturday December 15, 2023 I went to church at BVT Outreach Ministries like I have for almost twenty years. Little did I know that God would show up that day and for those who would respond "yes" to an invitation that would be given by the Pastor to be a part of something brand new. You see, that day Pastor, Overseer, Teacher and Author Dr. Marci Tilghman Bryant shared that in 2016 God spoke to her in a dream to write her next book entitled True Tides, that was seven years ago.

Which tells me that when God speaks and gives us instructions to accomplish something that we are not to be discouraged when things don't happen when we believe they should? In the Book of Genesis which also means beginning in Chapter 5:32 tells us that Noah was over 500 years old when he fathered his sons. In Genesis 6:14 God told him to build the ark. God told him what materials to use and how to design it, He told him who to take, his sons, his wife and his son's wives to escape the waters of the flood. God even told him to take two of all living creatures, male and female to keep them alive. Genesis 6:22 says Noah did everything just as God commanded him. When God speaks to those who are His, He expects obedience and trust knowing that He is capable of filling in the gaps. So Noah was in his 500s when God told him to build it and yet Genesis 7:6 (says} Noah was six hundred years old when the floodwaters came on the earth. Therefore no matter how long it takes to complete a work, if God speaks it, we are to be about our Father's business and begin until God brings it to completion. God told Dr. Bryant to write the book and yet God didn't allow for the publication until years later. Why because He didn't intend for her to create the work alone. God allowed for six other writers to be a part of the finished product. True Tides consist of seven authors and in the Bible the number seven often symbolizes completion. Now is the time that God would say the book is ready.

You see years ago when she gave birth to True Tides she didn't even know some of the people who would make a contribution to the book, but God knew each one and for His purpose wanted those unknowns to be known through this body of work.

There are too many people who don't believe they have anything to contribute to the world. There are too many who feel hopeless and who feel like they have no worth. That certainly is not the will of the Father.

Remember Genesis 1:26 tells us that God made us in His image.

Please think on that, you and I are made in the image of God. We are made in His likeness, and He created us to be His workmanship. God said everything He created was good. He created us to do great works.

Some of those works aren't manifesting because the enemy of our souls has slithered into the lives of God's people bringing deceit therefore causing distrust and disobedience to the one who loves us unconditionally.

God created Adam, God gave Adam dominion, God had fellowship with Adam, God spoke to him, gave him everything he would need and warned him what not to indulge in because entertaining what was forbidden would cause heartache and pain. How many times have we gone against the True Tides and ended up living with regrets? True Tides to me is to live in sync with God. It is to live according to the wisdom of God, God said His word is true and anyone or anything that opposes His word is a lie. Satan is the father of lies. When Adam and Eve disobeyed God it opened the door to destruction. There is nothing new under the sun; the same is true for us if we choose to lean to our own understanding and fail to acknowledge God in all our ways then destruction will be on our path.

As it happened in Genesis 4: 6-7 the Lord said to Cain, "Why are you angry? Why is your face downcast? 7 If you do what is right, will you not be accepted? But if you do not do what is right, sin is crouching at your door; it desires to have you, but you must rule over it." A door is a point of entry and exit, so we have the power to open the door and close the door to sin. If we don't learn to master sin through the power of God's spirit then sin will become our master making us a slave. Sin will steal your peace, joy, money, youth, and your time leaving you feeling empty and distraught.

Psalm 31:15 tell us that our life and times are in God's hands. We are to be stewards over what He has entrusted to us. He gives us 24 hours each day. Some of that time is to care for our basic needs like sleep, eating, and earn a living. Since Jesus attended a wedding and there were celebrations of festivals in the Bible, I don't believe God is opposed to us having a good time with family and friends. He just doesn't want us to neglect the time we are to spend with him.

Matthew 6:33 says seek ye first the Kingdom of God. You see when we spend intimate time with the Father, He gives us the ability to conceive new ideas, businesses, ministries, songs, and in this instance a book. So here we are about to enter into a new year and for those who are a part of this project are going to be authors. It may have taken eight years for this book to be published but you see it was in God's timing because eight is the number of "New Beginnings".

So since you are reading this book True Tides then God must be speaking "New Beginnings" for you. The book started out with God speaking to one woman and again God spoke to her and said now I want you to invite others along for the journey.

The time has come, continue to draw nigh to God and He will draw nigh to you because He wants to use you. He wants someone else to be blessed through you. Ask yourself are you the one, God is seeking to help others live the life of abundance that God has designed for them? I hope your answer is yes, if so listen for the voice of God, obey and God will do the rest.

My prayer is that you will enjoy the love and labor of every word that has been written in this book to encourage you to begin or if necessary to begin again!

Joshua 1:9 have I not commanded you? Be strong and courageous. Do not be afraid; do not be discouraged, for the LORD your God will be with you wherever you go. Let the True Tides of God's word, love, mercy, and Spirit lead, guide, teach, and uphold you when you're feeling sad or tired and most importantly replenish, and strengthen you every moment of every day as you live your life to the fullest, helping others and bringing glory to His name.

In His Loving Service

Perspective #7 - *Pastor Sylana Christopher*

Exceptionally written with divine wisdom knowledge and grace God certainly guided the mind and hands of Dr. Marci, as she created this masterpiece titled "True Tides.

We all have experienced the ripple effect of waves in our lives. Many of us tried jumping over the waves as we saw them coming. Some of us were so distracted by other things and people that we didn't see nor know the waves were upon us until we felt the impact of them. Then there are some of us that just allowed the waves to take us wherever it did with no concern on where we would land. We just flowed with the waves carelessly, hopelessly and even in some cases wishing it would overtake us and we'd drown. We had given up on ourselves and wanted our lives to end. BUT GOD! He didn't allow it. He had a plan for our lives.

It's an amazing thing how at night when it's dark outside the waves in the water grown bigger and are called tides. It reminds me of how we go through dark periods in our lives and experience trials and tribulations. What we do in those moments and the decisions we make will predict our life's outcome. Will we allow the tide to take us under or will we swim against the tide to save our lives? Our response is critical. Thank God, that there's always a form of light in dark places. We thank God for the moonlight, that guides us through the night. During the day when the sun is shining bright, the tides are calmer. They are mererly waves and it's much easier to swim. I must be clear and say, I'm grateful for the tides that I learned to swim against. It's the tide that taught me how to survive. When I made the decision that no matter how hard I was hit. ...... no matter how much the tide was doing it's job to overcome me, my life has purpose. I have an assignment to complete and I have to do my job and survive in order to do so. I had to swim against the tide. I overcame because I can do all things with Christ that strengthens me. The decisions we make in life will either take us to our destiny or to a desolate place.

"True Tides" Thank you Dr. Marci for allowing God to use you to enlighten us all about our life's journey. This is definitely a must read.

Chapter One

LEARN TO DISCERN

The enemy of your soul and mine as well as the entire human race uses fiery darts to attack your progress in moving forward. This is because the lives that you are to pour into are ahead of you, not behind you.

Thus, his method of the firey darts is designed to stop you one day at a time; one step at a time until one day will be your last day. Ultimately he, the devil, wants to interfere greatly with your impact by keeping you still or turning you back to a past that only exists now in your memory.

Progress will require that you move forward, not backward.

ACTIVITY ONE

The enemy of your soul uses " fiery darts" to attack your freewill and your decisions to move forward positively with your life's purpose and life's goal.

You need to know these darts by name and once you recognize them you must extinguish them.

Dart# 1: The Toehold
Dart# 2: The Foothold
Dart # 3: The Stronghold

DART #1 - The Toehold

What entertains you, makes you smile from the outside in? What sends pleasure to your senses? What makes you loose yourself into a world where all problems *and* anxieties just seem to drift away?

LIST THEM ... DON'T BE SHY ABOUT IT ... LIST THEM HERE

1._____

2._____

3._____

4._____

5._____

6._____

7._____

8._____

9._____

10._____

Many of us can think of at least 10 things that have that kind of effect on us. Now that you have taken the time to list them here, go back and highlight the first 3 that would be the most desired to the last to be desired. List them in three boxes below in the order of the first one you would find the most difficult to walk away from:

Now think about them. What stands out as "positive"? How can you enjoyment and participatirig in this activity help others and glorify God?

Also how can your enjoyment and participating in each of these activities be viewed as "negative", taking your mind and service away from helping others or bringing glory to God? Don't rush this process. Respond to it seriously. It will make a great deal of difference in the lives that YOU have been chosen by God to touch and guide into the Christian experience.

Once you have allowed yourself to see the negative side of these actions you can now understand why the enemy, satan will only attack you in these areas because he sees them as your weakest, (a blind spot) and most volnerable. He does not want to wrestle with you in the areas where you are the strongest. Remember, he only wants to win, by pulling you away from your assignment(s) or stopping you from going forward; in other words ... stand still and stand stuck.

What is most appealing about those items you just listed?

_____

_____

_____

_____

_____

_____

_____

_____

_____

_____

_____

_____

_____

_____

_____

_____

_____

What spoke to you the loudest?

_____

_____

_____

_____

_____

_____

What stood out above all else?

_____

_____

_____

_____

_____

_____

Let's Pray:

My eyes Lord
Help me to see what I need to see ...

My ears Lord
Help me to hear what I need to hear ...

My touch Lord
Help me to touch what I need to touch ...

My smell Lord
Help me to smell what I need to smell...

My taste Lord
Help me to taste what I need to taste ...

OH TASTE AND SEE THAT THE LORD JS GOOD ...

At any one time all of these senses will play a role (or have played a role) in the things that attract you. If what attracts leads to negative or less than desirable circumstances; you hold the key, by your will, to change your thoughts, and ultimately change your direction. Thoughts lead to action.

Now, from what you have listed in what entertains you, is there one or more items that you would like to change or eliminate? If the answer is yes, just know that you can do it. It starts with your will and your prayer concerning the matter.

Dear Lord,

Help me become transformed by the renewing of my mind. I ask this because it would bring glory to you, and open new doors that I should open and new paths that I should follow. I want to be continually be led by you and blessed by you.

In Jesus Name

In keeping with your dreams and goals what would you like to have in your life to entertain you... that something that would cause you great joy and be pleasing to God ...

_____

_____

_____

_____

_____

_____

_____

_____

_____

_____

_____

_____

_____

_____

KNOW THIS!

You can have what you desire.

Delight yourself in the Lord and He will give you the desires of your heart *Psalm 3 7:4*

Action: Include one activity that you know pleases God, according to His word, and incorporate it into you life today and practice it everyday until it is apart of you.

DART #2 Foothold

Who do you admire above anyone else?

Why?

Admiration can be very destructive to one's spiritual growth and maturity if misapplied. While it's been noted that good and bad lie within us all. One of the true tests of character has to do with listening to what a person says and then watching what he/she does. Talking about what you have heard or learned along the way is quite different from what you act out or walk out in life. Many are brave until they come face to face with taking a stand. Cowards from the heart find it hard to follow through on what they say even when exposure is eminent.

Write down some admirable qualities that you see in others and then jot down how the devil might attempt to use them against you.

_____

_____

_____

_____

_____

_____

_____

_____

The word tells us that we should know them that labor among us. I recall in the book of Acts that many followers of Jesus via the apostles and disciples were asked to sell their worldly possessions so that they would all exist and share in common their needs as they made known the gospel to the public. Many made this sacrifice but there was a husband and wife who agreed to sell what they owned for the support of the early church and we read that story and Acts chapter 5 but instead of turning everything over to the church as they had agreed they chose to hold something back. For themselves. It seemed an admirable thing to do, however it was not. They lied. They agreed to something that they did not do and tried to cover the lie. You cannot lie to the Holy Spirit. This infraction cost them their lives.

Take a poll of a few friends and/or relatives. Ask them what do they see as admirable traits of character in you. However do this after you create a list according to your perception of you.

Create your list:

_____

_____

_____

_____

_____

_____

_____

_____

Now do your poll

_____

_____

_____

_____

_____

Are any of the responses the same?

_____

_____

_____

_____

_____

How do you personally feel about the responses?

_____

_____

_____

_____

_____

The Foothold

What are you most likely to give into when you are tempted more than a few times? (whatever it is would have already been identified on your "toehold" list.)

Have you ever allowed yourself to know that you can remove yourself from that particular temptation?

Think about it for a moment. What are some of the things that you can do that would remove yourself or the temptation away from you?

List them here and now ...

_____

_____

_____

_____

_____

_____

_____

_____

_____

Remember, you have the power within your freewill NOT to give into whatever would pull you away from the good things in life.

Speak the following to your soul:

I'm crucified with Christ; nevertheless I live; yet not I, but Christ lives in me; and the life which I now live in the flesh, I live by the faith of the Son of God, who loved, and gave Himself for me. H died so that I could live eternally without fault or blemish. Christ is my life, and I dwell in Him in the realm of His divine love. Therefore, I am free from sin, death, and the law, and any worldly tie that would attempt me to pull me from His side. I am a partaker of His divine nature and I do not have to all this "thing" to control me. I, in Christ Jesus, control "it" ...

Identify IT, and denounce IT!

_____

_____

_____

_____

_____

_____

_____

_____

_____

List some activities that you have long had an interest in but never pursued.

_____

_____

_____

_____

_____

_____

Perhaps now is the time to pursue a new hobby, a new direction in your life. You can do this! God is with you.

_____

_____

_____

_____

_____

_____

_____

Remember, the devil, who is the enemy of God and of your soul has a strategy. It is so important to him to tempt you into making a decision, immediately. DO IT NOW. That demonic force does not want you to take any time to think about your action, or the consequences of your action.

So when you feel pulled in a direction that you know inwardly is not right for you or that will bring shame to you and will rob God of His glory in you life ....

STOP .... WAIT .... DO NOT GIVE IN. PRAY ...

Dear God,

I am making progress because you are in control. Your word is the light unto my path and the lamp to my feet. I trust you to strengthen me in this area as I consciously remove myself away from the temptation.

Give me this day everything I need to overcome in this area of my life. By faith I walk away now and expect my good reward to come from you.

In Jesus Name

TODAY IS A SPECIAL DAY!

Today you will take notes on every aspect of your day from beginning to end.

Starting with your wake up in the morning to your lying down tonight, document your walk and your actions and interactions. Record them in this journal as they occur.

If you can't jot them down immediately, do so as soon as you can.

6AM
7AM
8AM
9AM
10AM
11AM
NOON
12AM

1PM
2PM
3PM
4PM
5PM
6PM
7PM
8PM
9PM
10PM
11PM

MIDNIGHT

EXTRA NOTES:

What if anything will you consider making some changes for the better?

_____

_____

_____

_____

_____

How will you make those changes?

_____

_____

_____

_____

_____

How soon will you start?

_____

_____

_____

_____

Dart #3: Pleasure

We as humans were given the right to enjoy our environment and the company of one another. We can find joy in music, singing, art, cooking, traveling, macramay, work etc. any number of good things.

But there is always that one who hates God and us so much so that he chooses to interfere with our thought processes to taint the true pleasure and undergird it with mayhem and sinful consequences.

<u>Stronghold</u>

When your desires pass the toehold and then the foothold you will arrive at the stronghold.

DART #4: Greed & Selfishness

Rarely you will get anyone to admit to being greedy and/or selfish. Greed, according to the scriptures carries with it heavy penalties. Greed unchecked becomes a slavemaster to sin. Greed feels like freedom, because it gives a false sense of power. It only leads to separation from loved ones and a life of neglect and loneliness, for the bible says they will fall (prov 11:28). Greed interferes greatly with a person's integrity. Any financial increase obtained through greed will dwindle away. (prov 13:11). Greed ruins a good reputation. "A good name is more desirable than great riches; to be esteemed more highly than silver or gold." Prov: 22:1.

Greed is the opposite of generosity. It is always generosity which always brings blessings. Wouldn't you rather walk in blessings than to always live in the uncertainty of what greed and selfishness will surely bring to your life?

Chapter Two

PRAY OVER YOUR SENSES

You have a powerful weapon. It's called prayer!

When we were created, God gave us 5 senses to be used to help us through life. He gave us eyes, windows to our environment, ears to hear within our environment, touch, both physical and non-physical, smell as both aromatic and comfortable as well as alarming and foul as a state of warning, and taste. Our taste are not just limited to foods but to our likes and dislikes which help shape our image.

Our senses need to be monitored and cared for. Every component of our lives is significant. So to this end we must not neglect our senses; we must pray over them ... the whole of you needs to be in tune with God.

My Eyes: Lord, help me to see what I need to see, not just want I want to see. Help me see in the natural as well as in the spiritual, the seen and the unseen. Then send the clarity of the images to by brain to be analyzed and identified so that I may rightly divide false from truth.

My Ears: Lord help me to hear what I need to hear, what you would have me to hear, not just what want to hear. Help me to discern truth from lies and adjust my actions accordingly.

My Sense of Touch: Lord help me to touch what I need to touch physically and emotionally and spiritually; not just what I want to touch seeking only intimate satisfaction. Allow me to touch lives for good, for greatness, for growth and positive change.

My Sense of Smell: Lord help me to sniff out and recognize what I need to so that stench and offensiveness does not attach itself to me in such a way that it causes avoidance from that which is meant to be good for me. Draw me away from stench (the stench of lies, wrong doing, stealing, lust, sin etc.} as it is offensive to you oh, thus, make it also offensive to me.

My Sense of Taste: Help me Lord to taste what I need to taste knowing that everything that seems good for my body is not good for my health. Change the pleasure pleasing tidbits for the healthy and vital nutrition that keeps me active and alert.

Any thing in either one of these senses is found not to be pleasing to you Oh God, help me to discern it and give me the desire to please you and not the tide of my flesh ...

Continue your prayer

_____

_____

_____

_____

_____

_____

_____

_____

_____

_____

_____

_____

In Jesus Name.

No longer do you have to be the target of the darts aimed at your senses. God Himself has delivered by His word and the blood of Jesus.

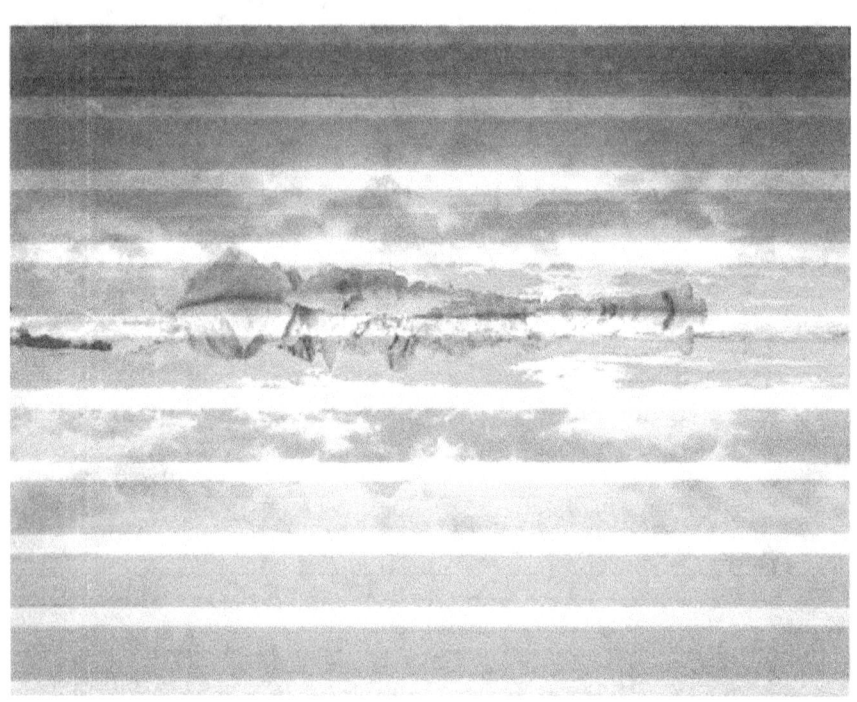

Chapter Three

THREE QUESTIONS

1. What am I good at?

2. For What purpose did God Create me?

3. What is my mission in this life?

God has the answers to these questions and your task is to retrieve them. Read Rev 6:8.

Where will we put our faith? Read Matt 9:28-30

God's word states: As long as the earth remains, there will be seedtime and harvest. Read Gen 8:22

God's Word States: Do not worry about your life. Reade Matt 6:25-34

God's word states: Worship the Lord your God. His Blessing will be upon you. Read Exodus 23-25

God's Word states: Do not fear; I am with you. Read Isa 41:20

God's Word states: Peace I leavem with you, not as the world gives. Read John 1427

You and I are called to live in hope and give hope through and by Jesus Christ. We can share what Jesus has done for us and our loved ones.

We can show the love that Christ has shown us by showing love to others. Often times in this world people are asking repeatedly for money when what they really need is to be shown the love of Christ. People need a hope and a faith walk that can only from God through Christ Jesus. You and I & all other Christians are this light that shines to show them the way.

Chapter Four

PURSUE GOD

Life calls us every day we wake up. Life also makes demands of us. Depending upon your environment and your outlook toward life, this will determine how you respond to these demands.

You will either meet the challenges by involving yourself or resist the challenges by removing yourself. If you neither resist or involve yourself, you stand stagnant, and, will rot where you are. And you will run the risk of becoming ineffective and repulsive, Sounds harsh doesn't it? The good news is that you can do something about it ... you can pursue God!!!

Allow me to offer you 6 keys in this journey.

KEY #1: PERSISTANCY. Read Matt 5:44 - Being persistent will bring results, praying during this time helps tremendously. You see time does not stand still. It moves and moves and moves. At some point you must realize that what is past is past, left behind and only exists in our memories. It's whatever is ahead of that still has the opportunity to make great impact. Stay the course.

KEY #2: PATIENCE. Read Psalm 37:7 - Hurried actions and decisions are not always wise. When pursuing God one must learn to wait for His responses to your hearts cry. Yes there is a right that seems right for man to travel but we must remember that we have an enemy that will camaphlog whatever he can to cause us to take the wrong path or to make a mistake in our reasoning of a situation. The enemy yells at us and pressures us to make quick, irrational decisions, while God gently guides to the path that is right for us. Patience one of the true keys to hear from God, as His response will always line up with His word.

KEY #3: PEACE. Read Phil 4-6-7 A relationship with God from your heart will always encounter peace. He gives us a peace that defies human understanding. While chaois might be all around us, we can be calm and reasonable in the mist of a storm. Having peace helps us rest and surrender to that which is good for our mind, body and spirit.

KEY #4: PRAISE. God inhabits the praises of His people. It sets the stage to come before Him. There are seven types of praise ...

Number one is HALAL. .. this praise is boastful and loud you can even look silly while you're doing it but you won't really care ...

The second type of praise is BARAK where you bow down on your knee before the Lord allowing yourself to be at his feet, humbly before Him ...

A third praise is TOWDAH ... this praise is with your hands outstretched in agreement to whatever God has said in his word, which is the same yesterday, today and forever. ..

then there's a fourth type of praise, ZAMAR ... to sign with instruments to just shake them and just play them, tap on them and blow them whatever the instrument calls for ...

Number 5 is TEHILLAH ... this is vocal singing out loud singing out long just singing from your heart ... from your heart to God's ear, sometimes in tears ...

Then there's a 6th type of praise ... SAVACH ... this is dignified praise lofty and loud as a battle cry like I got the victory, I thank you Lord, I thank you Lord ...

and then there's YADAH; last mentioned here but certainly not the least ... this praise is Wide Open ... publically you are declaring praise to God with your hands extended and adoration with your hands casting forward to God forward to the heavens forward to where God can see that you are looking only to him the author and finisher of your faith. Your hands move, your body moves all toward God.

Praise is so important for God's people ... it must and should be a part of our daily lives. He lives in the praises of his people. Give God His Praise daily.

KEY #5: PRESS. Read Phil 3:13-14

Tides flow seemingly effortlessly throughout its watery journey, however there are times when the winds are raging. There are times when the temperature is far below normal range. There are times when the sun is so hot that it can and does cause heat strokes to many humans. But still tides continue to move through its course.

Mankind is not always so committed or determined to keep moving in the right direction when incidents appear to make the course harder and more difficult to keep flowing. Often they look for an easier way out or an excuse to sit still or turn around ... reverse the course. This certainly is not always the wisest thing to do, even when the going gets rough. God promised us that he would be with us always, even unto the end of this age. We can choose to believe Him and PRESS on in the direction He has called us to travel or we can choose to believe in ourselves or the devil and stop pressing toward the intended mark of the Highest calling. You are not on the pathway alone. The power and the fortitude necessary for this journey is beside you every step of the way.

KEY #6: POWER. You shall receiver power from on HIGH ...

KEY #7: OVERTHINKING. The longer you think on a thing, the longer it takes you to make a decision. You can think yourself out of doing what is right ... what you know from the heart you have been called to act upon.

Chapter Five

FINISH WELL

A purely fantastic goal would be for you and I to walk forward every day in the newness of life utilizing the principles set by God to open the doors to blessings, allowing them to flow into our lives and the lives of others. Not only to walk into blessings every day but we want to declare and command ourselves to be a blessing. Someone needs your hand, your heart, your forgiveness, your understanding, your support, your knowledge, and wisdom that you have acquired from God.

Don't settle for finishing halfway through this mission. If you do settle halfway your will short change all the good you had in store for your life. Don't settle for just enough. Remember you want to be a blessing and to be a blessing you must have more than enough. More than enough comes to you only through the Father of Lights. He has made it possible for your cup to overflow daily.

I bring to your attention that Noah was called by God for a specific assignment. It was something that had never been done. He became the subject of constant ridicule, but his allegence to God was steadfast.

Year after year he stayed at his task. He built that ark according to God's specifications. No doubt he tried to explain to the many onlookers and mockers that "rain" was coming. But no one would take heed. Noah could have walked away from this task, afterall he had no support except for his family. But we know the end of this thing ... Noah finished well. He and his family and many of the animals were saved from the flood.

In the New Testament, one of the thieves on the cross, finished well. He had done nothing in life for which he could boast about or be proud of and now he had found himself on a cross sentenced to death. The only thing he had going for him was that he believed in God; he believed that Jesus had a kingdom and that He had come to the earth to save others which included him. His words were "when you come into your kingdom, remember me". Jesus' response was "Today you will be with me in paradise."

Jesus had a divine job to do. Although much came against Him, He chose to remain true to his call; true to His tide.

It's important for you to believe that you can and will finish well. For the truth is, whatever you believe you will always act on. This world can only offer you so much, but in Christ, we have so much more. We can't always see it with our naked eye but we can see it from our spirit, and believe it from the depths of our very soul. You can finish well!

www.ingramcontent.com/pod-product-compliance
Lightning Source LLC
Chambersburg PA
CBHW070938120626
46546CB00004B/1463